MEDITATIONS WITH™ ANIMALS:
A Native American Bestiary

from the voices of

Creek, Natchez, Chickasaw, Winnebago, Haida, Tlingit,
Kwakuitl, Zuni, Navajo, Apache,
Santo Domingo, Sioux, Osage,
Anasazi

Collected & adapted by
Gerald Hausman

Illustrated by
Liese Jean Scott

Foreword by Thomas Berry
Afterword by Dr. Michael W. Fox

Bear & Company
Santa Fe, New Mexico

This book is for Lorry, who waited
while things waited while things
were getting done.

Bear & Company, Inc.
P.O. box 2860
Santa Fe, NM 87504

Design: Katherine Ade
Illustrations by Liese Jean Scott
Typography: Casa Sin Nombre, Santa Fe
Printed in the United States by BookCrafters, Inc.

Contents

Foreword: Returning to Our Native Place

We are returning to our native place after a long absence, meeting once again with our kin in the earth community. For too long a while we have been away somewhere, entranced with our industrial world of wires and wheels, concrete and steel, and our unending highways where we race back and forth in unending frenzy.

The world of life, of spontaneity, the world of dawn and sunset and glittering stars in the dark night heavens, the world of wind and rain, of meadow flowers and flowering streams, of hickory and oak and maple and spruce and pineland forests, the world of desert sand and prairie grasses; and within all this the eagle and the hawk, the mockingbird and the chickadee, the deer and the wolf and the bear, the coyote, the raccoon, the whale and the seal, and the salmon returning upstream to spawn.

All this, the wilderness world recently rediscovered, with heightened emotional sensitivity, is an experience not too distant from that of Dante meeting Beatrice at the end of the *Purgatorio* where she descends amid a cloud of blossoms. So long a wait for Dante, so aware of his infidelities, yet struck anew and inwardly "pierced" as when, hardly out of his childhood, he had first seen Beatrice. The "ancient flame" was lit again in the depths of his being. In this meeting, Dante is describing not only a personal experience but the experience of the entire human community at the moment of reconciliation with the divine after the long period of alienation and of human wandering away from the true center.

Something of this feeling of intimacy we now experience as we recover our presence within the earth community. This is something more than working out a viable economy, something more than ecology, much more than Deep Ecology seems to be aware of or moved by. This is a sense of presence, a realization that the earth community is a wilderness community that will not be bargained with; nor will it simply be studied or examined or made an object of any kind; nor will it be domesticated or trivialized as a setting for vacation indulgence, except under duress and by oppressions which it cannot escape. When this does take place in an abusive way, a terrible vengeance awaits the human; for when the other living species are violated so extensively, then the human itself ceases to be a viable life form.

If the earth does grow inhospitable in such a manner and to such a degree, it is primarily because we have lost our sense of courtesy toward the earth and its inhabitants, our sense of gratitude, our willingness to recognize the sacred character of habitat, our capacity for the awesome, the numinous quality of every earthly reality. We have even forgotten our primordial capacity for language at the elementary level of song and dance wherein we share our existence with the animals and with all natural phenomena. Witness how the Pueblo Indians of the Rio Grande enter into the eagle dance, the buffalo dance, and the deer dance; how the Navajo become intimate with the larger community through their dry-paintings and their chantway ceremonies; how the peoples of the Northwest express their identity through their totem animals; how the Hopi enter into communication with desert rattlesnakes in their ritual dance. This mutual presence finds expression also in poetry and in story form, especially in the trickster stories of the Plains Indians where Coyote performs his never-ending magic. Such modes of presence to the living world we still carry deep within our selves beyond all the suppressions and even the antagonism imposed by our cultural traditions.

Even within our own Western traditions at our greater moments of expression, we find this presence, as in Hildegard of Bingen, Francis of Assisi, and even in the diurnal and seasonal liturgies. The dawn and evening liturgies especially give expression to the natural phenomena in their numinous qualities. Also, in the bestiaries of the medieval period we find a special mode of drawing the animal world into the world of human converse. In their symbolisms and especially in the moral qualities associated with the various animals, we find a mutual revelatory experience. These animal stories have a playfulness about them, something of a common language, a capacity to care for each other. Yet these movements toward intensive sharing with the natural world were constantly turned aside by a spiritual aversion, even by a sense that humans were inherently cut off from any true sharing of life. At best they were drawn into a human context in some subservient way, often in a derogatory way when we projected our own vicious qualities onto such animals as the wolf, the rat, the snake, the worm, the insects in all their admirable qualities. We seldom entered their wilderness world with any true empathy.

The change is begun, however, in every phase of human activity, in all our professions and institutions. Greenpeace on the sea and Earth First on the land are asserting our primary loyalties to the community of earth. Gary Snyder with his poetry and Paul Winter with his music are communicating with the entire span of natural beings. Paul Winter especially is responding to the cry of the wolf and the song of the whale in his music. Roger Tory Peterson has brought us intimately into the world of the birds. Joy Adamson has entered into the world of the lions in Africa. Dian Fossey has entered into the social world of the gentle gorilla. John Lilly has been profoundly absorbed into the consciousness of the dolphin. Farley Mowat has come to an intimate understanding of the grey wolf of North America. Others have learned the dance language of the bees. Even the songs of the crickets have been studied.

What is fascinating about these intimate academic associations with the various animals is that we are establishing not only an acquaintance with the general life and emotions of the various species but also an intimate rapport, even an affective relationship, with individual animals within their wilderness context. Names are given to individual whales. Indeed, individual wild animals are entering into history. This can be observed in the burial of Digit, the special gorilla friend of Dian Fossey. Dian's own death by human assault gives abundant evidence that we may be safer in the wilderness context of the animals than with humans in civilized society.

Just now one of the great historical missions of the primal people of the world is not simply to sustain their own traditions but to recall the entire "civilized" world back to a more authentic mode of being. Our only hope is in a renewal of those primordial experiences out of which the shaping of our more sublime human qualities could take place.

While our own experiences can never again have the immediacy or the compelling quality that characterized this earlier period, we are experiencing a post-critical naiveté, a type of presence to the earth and all its inhabitants that includes but also transcends that scientific understanding that now is available to us from these long years of observation and reflection.

Fortunately we have in the native peoples of the North American continent what must surely be considered in the immediacy of its experience, in its emotional sensitivities, and in its modes of expression: one of the most integral traditions of human intimacy with the earth, with the entire range of natural phenomena, and with the many living beings which constitute the life community. Even minimal contact with the native peoples of this continent is an exhilarating experience in itself, an experience that is heightened rather than diminished by the disintegrating period through which they themselves have passed. They are presently emerging as one of our surest guides into a viable future.

Throughout their period of dissolution, when so many tribes have been extinguished, the surviving peoples have manifested what seems to be an indestructable psychic orientation toward the basic structure and functioning of the earth, despite all our efforts to impose on them our own aggressive attitude toward the natural world. In our post-critical naiveté we are now into a period when we become capable once again of experiencing the immediacy of life, the entrancing presence to the natural phenomena about us. It is quite interesting to realize that our scientific story of the universe with its observational studies and analytical processes of inquiry into the story of the universe is more and more coming to appreciate these earlier stories that come down to us through peoples who have continued their existence outside the constraints of our civilizations.

In the collection of verse and story that follows, we are brought back into the primordial community of the universe, the earth, and all living beings. Each has its own voice, its role, its power over the whole. Each can take on the form of the others. But most important, each has its special symbolism. The excitement of life is in this numinous experience wherein we are given to each other in that larger celebration of existence wherein all things attain their highest expression. For the universe by definition is a single gorgeous celebratory event.

THOMAS BERRY
DIRECTOR
RIVERDALE CENTER FOR EARTH STUDIES
NEW YORK CITY

Preface and Acknowledgments

The poems, chants, and oral renditions in this book originally appeared as direct translations from interviews conducted for *The Bureau of Ethnology Reports*. I am particularly indebted to Reports 1-38. As with other books I have written where Bureau materials were used, this one uses a process I call *spiritings:* the deliberate attempt to reinvoke the spirit of the past without the intermediary of interviewer, anthropologist, or scholar. To the extent that my renewed spiriting works, I have much to be grateful for, but especially to those patient "field workers" who, mostly around the turn of the century, ventured forth to record the words of a culture that was fast disappearing.

When the spirit was right, the cooperativeness of the poem was in harmony with its origin—an oral story being told to someone. My constant thought on this project was to invest the past with the urgency of that past's *present.* So often in such renderings, the reader feels—this is *how* it happened but not *as* it happened. I have tried to put that necessary *as*, that contingency of the ghost that speaks, back in.

The author wishes to thank the publishers of the following books wherein some of his own writings first appeared: Copper Canyon Press for "Prayer for Red Meat" and "Dawn Stealer;" and Bookstore Press for "Skin Walker."

Grateful acknowledgment is also given *Waterways: Poetry in the Mainstream* for first publication of "Santo Domingo Corn Dance."

To the following persons the author wishes to extend personal thanks: Ray Brown for saying what Navajo was; Jim Smith for taking me to Choctaw; and Gerry and Barbara Clow for beasting-it-out with me.

INTRODUCTION

I

Our greatest bestiary is the Bible, and although this finest of oral documents speaks primarily about man, it is clear that the tellers meant to convey all of the unities that God intended. For instance, in Job, God responds to man "through the medium of all creatures real, or imaginary monsters like Behemoth or Leviathon." As bestiary author Dom Jean Leclerq, O.S.B. also states: God's creativity is not without humor; the creatures in Job are the playmates of God. Together, not apart, they celebrate the deeper mysteries of life.

In this sense, all creatures of God's earth, whether imaginary or real, share what should be man's devotion, his godliness. Again, as Leclerq says, "They are still his companions, even in fact his models."

This was the fundamental urge that brought our ancestors joy when they transcribed our original Book of Beasts, a book of science and religion, a book of imagination and fact.

From the toil of the teller comes all manner of elaboration. From the fireside, from the cliffwall, from the close and distant vibration of night. What goes, what stirs beyond the fire? In story after story, telling after telling, man remembers, rethinks himself, anew. What emerges is that other Adam, the four-footed winged member of a long-gone race.

It is not surprising that Native American storytellers eliminated the dichotomy of men and animals while striving to tell of their unique oneness with nature. You do not know in most Native American stories whether the protagonist is animal in raiment or spirit; or, if again, he might not simply be a naked man.

Native American tradition drives home the healing message—
we are of this world, not separate from it. Yet to travel in the
footsteps of the past, we must suspend our beloved scientific
reason and walk in the momentary magic of what I should like
to call illogic.

In the words of Navajo spokesman Ray Brown: ". . .What white
people insist on calling *myths* is our *religion!*"

In harmony with his remark, I feel we must walk the road Black
Elk saw in his vision, the road of healing where all things, ani-
mate and inanimate, are inextricably joined. We must learn the
language of Native America and become a part of our own
natural history. Doing so, we will hear our universal heart—the
one God intended us to hear when the world was new.

II

One of the unique expressions of this Native American bestiary is the geographical span it encompasses. The territory which the first Americans called Turtle Island was a vast land of intricately patterned lakes, forests, deserts, plains, rivers, mountains and hills. A land as varied as its occupants were many. But, what many of us forget is the mobility of Turtle Islanders; how they moved, quickly and easily across the landscape, first on foot, then on horseback. Traveling for pleasure, for trade, for war, or for peace. Traveling because dreams told them something was waiting for them. Traveling because they had vision quests, moral missions. Traveling simply because they could; because the vastness of the land beckoned them to do so.

Another reason the first Americans moved about is that their brothers and sisters, the animals of Turtle Island, were also travelers. The Indians felt the same pangs we feel today when a flock of Canadian geese goes overhead or when driving at night on a lonely road in the South, we come across, unlikely as it may seem, a slippery migration of salamanders.

Across six directions the creatures traveled along their ancient migratory byways. Heavens turned, stars wheeled, animals moved. Native Americans were one with this movement, a part of their spirit. Following the established trails of wild animals, they carved routes which became in time pathways the white man would use for a more self-directed purpose.

Well known Native American tribal paths always led to water, saltlicks, or other primal places of shelter and food-source. Animals, in the legend-leavings of tracks, explained where the water was, whether it was sweet, brackish, or merely tolerable. Names of such tribal routes echo today with meanings both poetic and geographic: the Big Bone-Blue Lick Trail, the Chickamuga Path, the Natchez Trace, the Place Where Deer Are Shy, the Mud Place, the Place of Fear. Many of these names speak as clearly today as the red or brown petroglyphed hands on walls of caves and canyon stone. They say, elegantly, simply: *we were here, the People*. The Animals said it with hooves and claws. The People used their fingers and palms.

So difficult, now, to imagine a sprawl of time where landscape is unhindered for the purpose of travel. We tend to think of Native Americans as home-bodies, earth-people who would have no reason—before the white man—to move around very much. Such was not the case. Iroquois of the Northeast knew the Black Hills of the Dakotas. Creeks and Chickasaws knew the grass barrens of the Midwest, as did the rock-dwelling Hopi. An Indian man traveling with his son, moving along at a steady gait somewhere between a fast walk and a slow run, could cover 120 miles in fifteen hours. Geronimo, fleeing the San Carlos Reservation concentration camp with his band of followers (men, women and children, old and young), would cover approximately 250 miles in seventy hours.

Pipes of the Cherokee, blankets of the Pueblo, copper of the Great Lakes, shells and feathers of the coast—these gave good reason for taking to the trail. And this was itself inextricable from the rhythm of the animal self: Weren't pipes in the shape of water dwellers? Weren't blanket designs a reflection of the flight of birds? Weren't bowls covered by the traceries of the spider people? Amulets of medicine power came from skin, teeth, and bone; an animal taken on as spiritual advisor represented a lifetime of knowledge of that animal. Its ways and wanderings were identical to the shadow movements, to the merging life of a man.

What follows in this book is yet a further reflection of animal-man, bird-man, scaled-feathered-furred-man. I have tried to let the spirit out. To let the movement of poem and chant fly across the page. To let the creatures moving along those most ancient byways speak, not across divided nations or states, but across the weave of time.

AUTHOR'S NOTE

Hopefully it should be clear that such artificial designations as "People of the Plain" and "People of the Lake" are more poetical than factual. This is not to say these references are not helpful; they are, that is why I have used them. But they are not strictly accurate as any Native American scholar knows. For instance, many tribes lived by rivers; it was a good way to live. Woodland tribes might also be called, in some cases, mountain tribes. Desert people—Apaches, for instance—ranged vigorously about the mountains, the plains, and the deserts. Most tribes, in their own language, referred to themselves as *the People*, not *the People of*.

I also wish to add the following comment—the meditation passages in this book are quite literally meditations. They arose out of deep thought and were written in a trance-like state, which may account for their stylistic rhythm. Later I accurately researched and sometimes corrected the thread of my thoughts. I did not, however, alter their "voice."

PEOPLE OF THE RIVER

SPIRIT FEATHERS

Death feather of the crow
puts my enemy
to sleep

    Crow feather
    Crow feather

Life feather of the jay
makes my mind
awake

    Jay feather
    Jay feather

Peace feather of the crane
turns my enemy
into me

    White crane
    White crane

       Creek

MEDITATION ON SPIRIT FEATHERS

Black was the presence of all colors, and crows were the embodiment of the spirit presence of death in all things. The world of the Creek was inspired by death as a part of all things living. To the Native American death was not the end of life, but the cradle upon which new life depended. To envision black—the feather of death—was to see the momentary passing of an enemy. Night was the color of the crow, the suspension of life, the moment before the coming of dawn. The crow as carrion-eater, like the raven, was a part of Indian cosmology; a cleaner, in a sense, of the "negative image" of death. The Creeks were known to imbibe a black emetic whose purpose was to flush clean the inner system and purify them; like the eating of a crow's feather.

Blue was the color of the sky and earth-nourishing waters—lakes, rivers, rain—the female presence, female life-giving essence, yin. Blue water was the ritual of awakened or reborn self; bathing in blue was baptismal. The Creeks knew that a black feather in the mind of an enemy would put him to sleep, symbolically kill him. A blue feather would revive the spirit of one who was placed under the spell of blackness. The bluejay, cousin to the crow in scapegrace ways, possesses another side: full of life, scraper on the nerves of those who don't live to the fullest.

White was the absence of color, beyond the power of blue or green. The crane, which can stand on one leg, is a meditator in the stream of time, taking what comes as it may. The principle of unworried and unhurried nature is the crane. With mantle of snow, the white crane symbolizes divine wisdom—not life reborn—but life-everlasting, nirvana.

WARNING OF THE OWL

A man asked: O'pa the owl,
Do you call when someone's dying?

O'pa the owl said: Hoorooooo

The man asked: O'pa the owl,
Do you call when someone's lying?

O'pa the owl said: Hoorooooo

The husband said: O'pa the owl,
Do you call when a wife's crying?

O'pa the owl said: Hoo

The hurt husband said: I hear now
Someone sighing, someone sighing.

O'pa the owl said: It is your wife
Sleeping with another man.

Creek

MEDITATION ON OWL

We think of the owl as a mysterious harbinger. Native American belief was less romantic, less mysterious. The owl called, you prepared to die. Nothing of the occult in this; more like plain fact, unadorned truth. The Pueblos of the Rio Grande have a healthy respect for the owl, so much so that they will not enter a house where owl feathers or the body of an owl have been mounted. The owl is feared and respected. While death, as mentioned in the commentary on "Spirit Feathers," is not a matter of trepidation, it is a matter of utmost seriousness. In "Warning of the Owl," the message shows that infidelity was borne by the same messenger who brought news of death. The correlation between death and sexual transgression is significant.

CALLING OUT DEER WOMAN

Anything that will charm a deer
will charm a woman.
White, blue, red, yellow—
they luster like glass,
the little sabia crystals.

Look out, they're alive!
Look out, one jumped three feet
into the air!

Sing the long song now,
a little piece of buckskin
tucked around your crystals.

Open them up, take a look.
Now put some red berry juice
on the end of a wheat-straw

and touch it to your cheek.
Now make the song
that sings the deer blind,

the sabia song to make them
stagger blind. In hunting
and in love the little sabia
give a man that which he should
not be refused.

Natchez

MEDITATION ON
DEER WOMAN, THE HUNT, CRYSTALS

A question was asked by a white man: How did Indians
know that one plant cured fever, another was poison?
As the poem says, they called it out; their wisdom was
reverent and reverberant. Draw a circle. What lies
within is the world. The circle in this poem is the spiral
of love; love of fleshly woman, love of the flesh of the
deer.

The healing value of crystals is known today as it was
during medieval times. That they possess life is not a
surprise given the endless circle of existence, the animism of the Indian. The poem uses the power of love
to call the deer out of hiding, to have it stand, as a
naked lovelorn woman, "blind in love." In love we are
blind to death. The deer in the hunt and the woman
chosen by the lover are courted from the same dark
root of desire. This is the desire for life, not death. The
hunt: a celebration of the hunter, the continuing life of
the deer. The circle continues. The line: ". . . that
which he should not be refused." Just as the circle may
not be broken, the desire or will—in pure form (not
carnal form)—is necessary for life. It is unselfish to
wish, to dream, to hunt.

THE HORNED SNAKE

Horned Snake, My sister!
Horned Snake, My brother!

Take me to your snake towns,
Give me your magic cane!

Show me the way to your sacred cave!

Horned Snake, make me the hunter
my grandfather was
with his name Yabi Odja,
      Yabi Odja!
With his string of turtles
      tied to his back
      held together
with hickory bark: Yabi Odja,
my grandfather, the hunter!

      Creek

MEDITATION ON YABI ODJA

A Native American spokesperson once went on record as saying that the snake people had made war on the white man because he had made war on them *first*. The snake that lives in the water with the head of a stag is not a "bad snake," but a powerful one. The difference here is between *power* and *evil*, *power* and *good*. Good and evil, according to the Navajo, are mixtures of quality; they may be used for either purpose in the name of power. People may wield power well, or with ill in mind. Or with well and ill purpose joined in a figure of power who clearly works for the well-being of all. Thus, the nature of good and bad are mixed. In one hand may reside good, in the other, bad. And yet the whole being, the man, may be good or bad or both as the situation demands. The unification of dualities is the word *power*. Power shares, does not isolate, does not belong to only *one*. Made of many, it may be held or withheld by many. One man may have more of it than another.

The snake in many tribes is a figure of duality joined. The Creek's Horned Snake possessed power to draw a deer to the river, transfix it with a stare, and drown it. Afterwards, it ate only the deer's nose. Hunters of the Creek nation used horn of the Horn Snake for hunting. The horns which looked like red sealing wax were broken into pieces and shared by many men on the hunt. The Alabama Indians called the Horned Snake *Tcinto sakto*, Crawfish Snake. The Creeks also knew the Celestial Snake which had a head, no body, lived on dew, and could spin into the air like a whirlwind. This snake combined the elements and powers of nature: good, evil, sacred, fearful. In the same way, the Horned Snake unified the hunter with the hunted: on its head, the emblem of the stag, that which is sought by the

Indian hunter. Its snakelike nature offering the ability to hypnotize.

Men who undertake to know the power of the snake must first recognize that it is a godlike being. The white man made—and still makes—war on snakes. The Native American reverenced the snake and would no more kill it without reason than kill a man without reason. When a white man kills an animal—a snake, for instance—he believes that the energy of the snake, its spirit, dies in death. That spirit may live on until—as the old belief tells us—the sun goes down. After that, the snake, with its presence of evil, is dead. Not so with the Native American. Snake spirit does not die in death, it returns to avenge its assailant.

The Horned Snake allowed its spirit to be borrowed for the unselfish communal purpose of the hunt. Yabi Odja had Snake-power because he was allowed into the sacred cave of the Horned Snake priests and he was given the ability to dive deeply and hold his breath long on turtle hunts. This is not unlike the Hopi story of Tiyo, the Snake Boy, who, taken into the underground kiva of the rattlesnake priests, was given a rattler-bride, who later bore him children. The Hopis did not mind this except their children were bitten, and so the snakes were driven out of Hopi in disgrace. As a result, a great drought came to the land, proving to the Hopis that the rattlesnake people controlled the cycle of rain. Today, this belief is enacted, as it has been for hundreds of years, in the celebrated Hopi Snake Dance, during which the trance effect of snake and man may be witnessed, but not necessarily explained. Man and snake become one entity; the shared power flows between the two in uninterrupted trance-like grace. When the snakes are released, they are returned to keep the balance they brought to men in nature, in their own world.

THEY CALLED THEM BIRDS

They lived high on a hill.
They were people who were up before
first light.
They did not have peculiar customs.
They would not bother anybody.

They were of the following minds—
    crows, hawks, horned owls
    field larks, hummingbirds
    blue birds, chickadees
    quails, woodpeckers
    yellow hammers, whippoorwills.

They did not work, they lived easy.
The best of them were wiser
than other clans.
They did not depend on anyone
but themselves.

They were the Bird Clan.

              Chickasaw

36

MEDITATION ON THE BIRD CLAN

Essence of the bird people: independence and happiness. Birds bicker and fight, soon forget. Do not hold grudges. The overall human concept of "bird" is flight, the presence of freedom. This poem appreciates a further freedom of the bird people: freedom from work. Do other animals work? The beaver is a worker, the wolf is incessantly on the prowl. When the hawk works, he does it with such comparative ease that we do not reflect upon it as work at all, but some kind of sky-like concentration. The bird people have it several ways at once: independence *and* each other. Day, in all its glory, early. Unbound by endless rituals, carefree. They live freely, yet do not seek to impose their freedom upon anyone else. The name Chickasaw is a bird sound. It whistles when you say it.

The nature of a clan insures several things, mostly spiritual identification. The representative of the Bird Clan of the Chickasaw had, not just his own and his clan's honor to look out for, but the entirety of the feathered world. In dance, in dress, in behavior, in custom this man was synonymous with the spirit-nature of bird. The honor that was *each* was also *other.* Only in a tightly bound way could man and creature transcend the notion of dualism. In the Chickasaw clan birds protected men and men protected birds.

In the Christian world, forgiven sin creates duality. In tribal clans, man's place did not permit dualized thinking. There is no variable to be obeyed or disobeyed. As in Taoism, no right or wrong, only the Way. A Choctaw man was expelled, not only from his clan but his tribe, for lying. They were the Bird Clan, no other.

THE PEOPLE

The people of the Southeast became known as the Five Civilized Tribes: the Cherokees, Choctaws, Chickasaws, Creeks, and Seminoles. Deriving originally from a branch of the Creeks, the Seminoles were the only tribe of the Five who did not sign a peace treaty with the white man. Early settlers among the Spanish and French observed that Indian chiefs were actually just like their own kings. In point of fact, the Native American "kings" were elected by the will of the people, not the grace of god. The social structure and political framework of the Southeastern tribes had a certain flavor of democracy to it which, no doubt, influenced the whites in their own governmental procedures.

It may be interesting to note that the color distinctions shown in the Creek poems could have been rooted in a designation made by the original occupants of their territory, the Muskogis. It was a Muskogi custom to divide villages or towns into white and red; white towns housed chiefs of state, while red towns housed chiefs of war.

The mystery of the Natchez people is of interest. They were called a broken tribe, even in the eighteenth century. They called themselves *Na tsi* and were indistinguishable in dress from the Cherokees. The French explorers called them Natches or Natchez, and their original settlement was along St. Catherine's Creek, east of the present city of Natchez, Mississippi—"One league from the shore of the Mississippy."

The "pure" race of Natchez Indians was considered a race of wizards and conjurers. But they lived with, not always harmoniously, the Creeks, the Chickasaws, the Catawbas in South Carolina, North Carolina, and Georgia. Explorers in 1900 called them Notchees and saw them as Cherokees because they lived in Cherokee County, dressed as Cherokees, and spoke the Cherokee tongue fluently.

Who were these people of mixed origin? Conjurers who lived off other tribes? Wizards who stayed alive because they knew the secret of being whatever their environment required in terms of language, dress, and behavior?

In 1708, the French explorer Du Pratz called these Indians not *Sauvages* but *naturels*. This Rousseauian distinction is uncharacteristic of other explorers. He also saw that their intrinsic rather than imitative beauty inspired as much "jealousy as admiration" among the tribes with whom they settled.

In 1907 there were five Native Americans alive in Braggs, Oklahoma who could still speak the original Natchez tongue. They were known to their white neighbors as Creek Sam, Wat Sam, Charlie Jumper, Lizzie Rooster, and Nancy Taylor.

It is not known today why certain historians of the Natchez people believe they were the last human remnants of the the lost island of Atlantis.

The Five Civilized Tribes, having settled and farmed and even run plantations just as the whites were doing, and creating the Cherokee alphabet so that reading and writing were not only possible but practical, were driven off their land between 1832 and 1839 and relocated in a foreign (to them) territory soon to be a state. They arrived in time to name it Oklahoma.

PEOPLE OF THE LAKE

THE ANIMALS GAVE FREELY OF THEIR MEDICINE

A man was going to die.
He went to the top of a hill and lay down.
Briefly he slept.
When he awoke there was a circle of animals.
Each animal gave the man his own personal
Medicine.

Raven said—e-he-a! e-he-a!
Then he spit on the man and gave of his own
Medicine.

The man felt better.

Turtle said—ahi! ahi! ahi! ahi!
Then he gave the man of his own boiled
Medicine.

The man felt better.

Black Hawk said nothing.
He gave the man of his medicine right on the place
Where the man hurt the most.

The man felt much better.

Then all the animals said—
"Human, in a similar way,
You will cure your fellowmen!"

And the man was given the Flutes of Power.
And he became a great Healer, a powerful
Medicine Man and it was because the animals
Gave freely of their medicine.

Winnebago

MEDITATION ON ANIMAL MEDICINE

All creatures had power, but some had more than others; Black Hawk goes directly to the source of illness, says nothing.

All things were used for medicinal purposes: leaves, bark, blossoms, and roots. The Winnebagos used toad and quail for poison. A dead person's heart might be mixed with that of a redbird for a healing potion. A bear's liver could be rubbed over the body to relieve pain. The entire body and brains of a raven could be used in healing. A rattlesnake could be used to help a woman whose child was "killed in the womb." Anything might be cured so long as the patient wished a cure. A wish, a dream, a prayer: one and the same. A Winnebago man might seek a way to gain earthly holdings through prayer and he might seek courtship of a woman through medicinal means. Spirit healing crosses the material plane: a belief of poverty seen as a belief of ill-spirit.

A Navajo said that a man deserted by the deities is one who "shows too much confidence." Such a person does not need deitific help. The Winnebagos said that only a "lowly person" is safe from the rancor of an evil shaman. A great medicine man—a prophet in his own land—inspires great jealousy. The best path is the middle way—neither high nor low, but in between. In healing, animals give freely of their medicine but only to the deserving. Not to those who think they deserve.

SONG OF SPIRIT GRIZZLY

I am he, I am he!
The day it is I.

You will be listened to—
you were told,
you were told—
you were told by the children
as many as there are.

The grizzly bear was starting to roam.

Shouting, you can hear him.
His voice, you can hear.

Winnebago

MEDITATION ON SPIRIT GRIZZLY

This song sung at a bear healing ritual or bear dance suggests the homage due Spirit Grizzly. All members of the healing ceremony are blessed by Grizzly Bear during fasting. In the center of the lodge where the bear dance will take place is a small mound representing a bear cave on top of which tobacco is placed. Dancers eat this tobacco and spin and whirl as bears do when they dance. The power of this dance on a wounded man corresponds to Cherokee Bear Chief's ability to reintegrate himself after death. Winnebago ritual tells of a wounded warrior who is unconscious. The dance given for him is done with the belief that he can heal himself if he remembers his Bear's blessing. The man's name is Little Priest. He lies on the floor of a lodge; his fingers begin dancing faintly as the bear people weave all about him. Tobacco and red feathers are placed on the Bear Cave Mound and in four directions. Bear people dance, hold out hands, supplicate, pray, offer power. Little Priest's fingers dance, then his whole arm. He sits up, rubs earth in his wounds. He seems to be in a trance. He stands and dances. First he moves weakly, then he dances with the bears, his power completely restored!

THE SHAMAN SPEAKS

I come from above and am Holy!

Once I was at war and was killed.
After my death I arose and went to my home,
but my wife and children would not speak to
me. Then I went back to the place where I had
been killed and saw my body. I tried to return
to the place where I had lived for four years,
but I was unsuccessful.

Once I was a fish. But the life of a fish is
much worse than ours. They are frequently in
lack of food. But they are very happy beings
and have many dances.

Once I was a little bird. When the weather was
good, I liked being a bird person. But in cold
weather I suffered from lack of food. I lived
in a hole in a tree. If I slept too far in,
I could hardly breathe and if I slept too far
out I was cold all night.

Once I was a buffalo. I had plenty to eat and
a warm coat of fur to keep me warm. But there
were always hunters and I had to be always on
the alert.

From my buffalo life I was permitted to go to
my higher spirit-home up above. There I met
Spirit Grizzly. I learned his songs so I
could sing them again back on Earth. I carried
a live coal in the palm of my hand and struck
it with the palm of my other hand. Then the
Spirit Grizzly fell to the ground and a black
ooze came out of his mouth. All the Spirits
said to me: "Fine, you have killed him, now it
is your task to return him to life." Then they
gave me a flute and a gourd and they cut Grizzly
into pieces and put a dark material on top of
him. Then we all breathed upon him four times
and the Spirit Grizzly got up in the shape of
a human being and lumbered away. The Spirits all
said, "Just as you have done here, you will do
down on Earth. You have the power to kill and to
restore. You have been blessed."

Winnebago

MEDITATION ON BEAR POWER

The power of the bear is implicit in Native American thought. Bears, though, have good and bad power. A spirit unruly and wild, human and divine. They may be that side of us which is inclined to do harm. In rites the bear is brought to earth in spirit, tamed by good wishes, good faith. Bear spirit is danced to, sung for, tobacco-sprinkled. Tobacco plant, sacred to Indians, is placed on the head of the bear. Given to the Directions, to the spirit of animal; tobacco as power.

The Cherokee story of Bear Man: a hunter lives with the bears and becomes one with them. Chief of all underground bears is white. Bear Man stays in the cave of bears all winter. Chief takes Bear Man to live with him, tells him in spring hunters will kill him (Chief) for meat and fur. Chief says Bear Man must make sure that after he is killed, his blood is covered with leaves. "When they are taking you away, you must look back over your shoulder and see something." It happens and when Bear Man looks over shoulder, he sees the Chief "rise out of the leaves, shake himself, go back into the woods." Bear Man, though his tribe "civilizes" him, tires of the world of men, dies. His bear nature is too strong. "Had they kept him shut up and fasting until the end of seven days, he would have become a man again, would have lived."

In this story, men do what they do and bears do what they do. The rite, however, must be done according to custom: leaves cover blood just so. Spirit of Bear returns if correct rite is observed; spirit of Man dies if correct rite is unobserved.

Power is borrowed, not stolen. Power given, not taken.

At what time, historically, the Winnebago entered Wisconsin is uncertain. They say their place of origin is Red Banks, near Green Bay. There is little doubt of their close relationship to such tribes as the Missouri, Oto, and Iowa. Iowa Chiefs stated that their people and those of the Oto, Missouri, Omaha, and Ponca once formed part of the Winnebago nation. According to them, they also came from the Great Lakes country of the Winnebago; however, the Winnebago stayed by the big waters because of the abundant fishing. When discovered by the French explorers in the early seventeenth century, the Winnebago were entirely surrounded by central Algonquin tribes: Menominee, Miami, Sauk and Fox, and Objibwa. Their nearest "kin" were in southern Iowa, western Wisconsin, and eastern Minnesota.

PEOPLE OF THE SEA

THE MAN WHO MARRIED A KILLER WHALE WOMAN

Every day a woman went to the point to gather
    mussels. At a certain place she beat
    upon her mat and a killer whale came up
    on the beach and made love to her.

Now one day the husband of the woman followed
    her to the point and saw what she did
    with the whale. Then he dressed himself
    in her clothing and sharpening a mussel
    shell into a knife, he beat the whale call
    song on her mat.

The killer whale lover flashed up out of the
    water to take his woman and his penis
    was hard and ready but the husband hid
    under his wife's blanket and he too
    was ready.

So the husband took out his mussel shell knife
    and he chonked off the whale lover's
    penis. Then the whale went away quickly
    making a noise.

That night the husband cooked the whale's penis
over a fire of coals and his wife came in
and said: "Oh, what is that you're cooking?"
"Something sweet," he said. So she took
a big bite of it and he asked: "Is your whale husband sweet?"

Then she ran outside and the ground shook and
she ran to the water and jumped in.

And the husband knew he had married a killer
whale woman born of human flesh and he saw
that her body turned into a reef when she
struck the water. That body, that reef, is now
called Woman.

Haida

MEDITATION ON KILLER WHALE

Animals are "entered" by humans in many ways;
dreams, visions, drugs, herbs; ecstasy of prolonged
exercise, as in dance; art wherein human hand makes
animal spirit live. In white culture such abilities or
talents are often considered god-given; they can only
be learned in the shamanistic sense if the bearer of
such talent, the artist, is first *born* into the condition of
learning. We say, the artist is a "born genius." This is
also true of the Indian world.

To eat an animal, to become one with its flesh, is to
know its essence. The Plains Indian hunter devours the
buffalo heart because of its inherent power or wisdom.
Cannibalism: the transference of power; to the
devourer goes the enemy's essential nature, his honor.

Another way of entering the animal is the doorway of
sexual penetration. Both cultures, white and Indian,
indulge in this entryway to the creative world. The tipi,
looked upon sexually, is both vagina and penis. In
shape and meaning: yin-yang, cone-circle, mother-
father, opening-thrusting energy.

Implicit in the Killer Whale Woman is male jealousy.
The man, in order to ensnare the lover and husband of
his wife, must wear her clothing, must sing the whale
call song on her mat. Therefore, he participates in her
ritual, shares her act with her creature mate.

This identification stops when he deprives the killer
whale of his penis. In the Haida description, little men-
tion is made of the whale's agony in this event, only
that he "made a noise." The man somehow still shares
the experience by softening the pain felt by the whale,

as if he too would have had that same pain. The animal identification yields a male-female interpenetrative stance. The story has a male tone to it but shares male-female feelings, human-animal life forces.

One of the great beauties and concomitant puzzles is the koan-like manner in which a Haida woman is actually Killer Whale Woman. She looks and acts as a human being would look and act, yet she is at heart a member of another race. This is accepted in the Indian world as it is not in the white world. Also accepted in the Indian world is the effortless way the story resolves: woman whose power is transcendent becomes something greater, becomes all-nature. Back to the sea, away from treachery; back to mother, back to beginnings. The reef, now called Woman: eternality, the female presence of all that nurtures. According to Haida belief, the reef known as Woman shakes whenever a human being sets foot on it. Supernatural beings do not want human beings walking on them.

KILLER WHALE WOOD

A Seal People Man
carved killer whales
out of hemlock,
    out of other wood.

He asked them to swim,
    they floated belly-up
        washed on the beach.

He used yellow cedar:
    he marked white lines
        from the corners of the mouth
        to the back of the head.

He said: "White Mouth Killer Whale,
            you will hunt seal and halibut
            but you will not hurt
            a human being."

And the Killer Whale went up the inlet
        and the people said:
            "Give us something to eat!"

                Tlingit

MEDITATION ON KILLER WHALE WOOD

Water, the sea, the female presence, fish, fish-animals—
all are of major importance in the Northwest Coastal
culture. What other element was of equal importance?
Wood. Along the coast the plentiful trees grew, offering
themselves as godlike presences that could, in proper
obeisance, be used just as the animals were given for
purposeful use, all things interchanging, nothing
excluded from this temporal and spiritual balance.

Along the coast: evergreens, spruce, fir, yew, redwood.
Best of all, most useful to all, the ever-workable cedar.
Canoes and houses made from cedar. Utensils. Bark
made into yarn, into clothing; a baby's cradle lined with
padding of cotton-pounded cedar. Naturally, the most
famous product of the Northwest Coast—the totem
pole, hierarchy and pantheon of gods in the form of
animal faces. These guardians stood totemically as ani-
mate art. The power passing from hand of man to
wooden animal is an active exchange of life.

In the poem, the carved animal is instructed to serve
humankind. The animal obeys. Hunting the coastal
waters, the killer whale drives fish into the nets and
spears of waiting men. The killer whale hunts fish to
live, but as instructed will not feed on men, nor even
hurt a man. They—humans and whales—are not in
competition with each other: in cooperative alliance.

The carved wood of the cedar canoe also has a life of
its own. It is not dead wood. The whale, carved by a
man who was also a god, possesses sensate intelli-
gence, but only when the man-god chooses the right
wood: yellow cedar. The law of utility is the law of
established ritual. Man is the borrower, beautifier; as
impermanent as all other transitory borrowers—killer
whales, fish, eagles, the ever-changing sea.

RAVEN'S BAG OF STARS

There was no light in the world
except in one
large house where a rich
man lived with his daughter. Together
they kept all
the light of the world.
Raven made himself into a small piece
of dirt
and dropped into their
drinking
water.
This made the rich man's daughter pregnant.
When her child was born it cried and cried.
The child wanted everything in the lodge
but especially the bundle bags on the pegs
of the walls of the rich man's lodge. The
daughter and her father gave the child anything it wanted and when it pointed to the
first bag it saw they handed
down a bag of stars.

The child took the bag and flung it
up into the air and the
bag sailed out
the smoke
hole
and that is how stars
came into the world.
From the next bag the child flung
the moon
and from the next one
daylight.
Then the spoiled child made Raven speech—
"Ga" it croaked
and then it flew up the
smoke hole
and was
gone
again.

Tlingit

MEDITATION ON RAVEN

Like Coyote, eternal trickster of plains and pueblos, swamps and woods, Raven is a birther of mischief. He is also a way-changer, shape-changer, way-shower. Coyote stole the sun and lost his eyes; Raven turned into a human baby star-thief, kidnapped a chief, and made himself into water. There is no end to either of these mischief-makers; even today in garbage dumps of America, they are seen cutting up the spoils, dyeing feathers and furs to suit the times.

A contemporary Coyote tale tells of a bushy-tailed wino living on the dark side of city streets, wearing black leather, sharing brew with his best buddy, Badger. Raven wears a silver-studded suit, cruises the plaza on his motorcycle. The image of the People as it is cast: always changing, suited to life as it is being lived. Coyotes and Ravens in jails, supermarkets, lost highways. Wearing stay-press suits, filling out forms for Uncle Sam. Shaping up new destinies by wearing old costumes, doing ghost dances, working up sweats, singing back the good old days.

EATING SALMON MEAT BY THE RIVER AT NIGHT

When a man takes salmon with hooks at night
he goes up river. He catches many salmon

and the people dry the roasted dog salmon
for the winter. But when they are speared

and not hooked, the river people at the mouth
of the river eat them while they still glow

with the shine of their skin. There are lots
of ways to eat salmon and these are only two.

Other ways are scorched salmon, blistered salmon
brittle salmon   cold roasted salmon
boiled salmon   old dried salmon
soaked green   salmon saved
salmon   in cellar
split-back   milky salmon spawn
salmon cheeks   mush of boiled
sun-dried   salmon head

When a man eats salmon by the river,
he sings the salmon song. It is in the river
in the roasting in the spearing in the sharing
in the shoring in the shaking shining salmon.
It is in the song too.

Kwakiutl

MEDITATION ON SALMON EATING

In Kwakiutl country, salmon was sacred. The spawning run: fish returning year after year, the same way spirits of the dead travel back to life. In the north country where certain game was scarce, fish and seafood became the sustenance of the tribe. With catch storable, leisure time was extenuated. One Native American's mental cookbook covered more than 150 different recipes. Even the boiled head was eaten, nothing lost, all returned from whence it came.

The cycle goes as follows: the basket wherein the fish is placed to boil (using a burning hot stone) is round as is the morning sun and the night coming after it. The roundness in the beaten bracelet, the song celebrating the making of the beaten bracelet, the catching of the beaten salmon. All return, like fish.

SWIMMER THE SALMON

I am the swimmer born deep in the gravel
of my mother's stream.
I come out of the dark in the spring
of the year and grow until my belly's
smooth.

I am the swimmer flying from shadows
that fly over me.
My enemies, eels and claws,
mouths and water-rings,
stilted feet of the shallows.

I am silver. I melt in the rush
of river rain, eat in the swift current
that tugs my fins.

I am the swimmer of first scars,
I swim and fall in my first long spillway
to the sea.

I enter the water of the moon, the great sea.
I the salt swimmer traveling winters,
tail growing, fins expanding.

One day
I breathe a secret smell,
taste the water of my home river.
Where does it come from?

I am followed by seals and porpoises.
Nets, traps, hooks await me,
seals and porpoises follow me.
Looking for my home.

Up current, no longer alone.
Brothers and sisters beating,
thrusting,
to the quiet pools behind rocks.
I am covered with scars.

Once, I sit in a bear's paw—
he drops me, fetches another.
We are many:
pushing and falling,
beating and climbing,
climbing steadily upward.

At last I am the swimmer who spawns.
Bruised and tired I cut
my bed in the sandy stones and wait.
Then I leave eggs deep in the gravel
of my home stream,
safe and deep,
moon-round like my journey.

When thunder comes, I melt away
in the rush of river rain.
Downstream, I am gone away.

Now I am swimmer who dies,
who runs with rain and moon and salt-wind tide,
river and falls and sweet pebble water.

Swimmer the Salmon
who always returns.
Swimmer the Salmon
who is always reborn.
Swimmer the Salmon
who comes with the moon.

Kwakiutl

MEDITATION ON SWIMMER THE SALMON

Atlantic salmon come up river as many as thirteen
times. Pacific salmon make it only once. Body spent,
tail silvering downstream from the river of birth, this
great fish is consumed by all kinds of predators.
Ignominious end—to the white mind—one-time shot
at life, consummated by utter loss.

The Pacific salmon lives briefly, dies briefly, yet lives
long in continual cycle of return. Kwakiutls saw the fate
of Swimmer as their own: fingerling moves downstream to the sea; spent male and female turn about
and die. Both swept to the sea. As you start, you end;
no difference. When a hunter of the sea died, the
Kwakiutls believed he went to the land of the killer
whale. When a land-hunter died he went to the home
of the wolves. A slave was sent to the home of the
owls. Twins born in a village were Swimmers. So it is
life is blessed with birth and death. A person alive is
always dying.

They were truly of the sea. The area they live in now is called the Northwest Coast and it covers a strip of land from the northern tip of California all the way up to British Columbia and Alaska. One edge of this landscape is coast bordered by seascape and on the other side is mountains. The climate is rainy and damp, the land itself shaggy and narrow, in places too narrow for the building of lodges. Yet the beauty of the Northwest culture for the Indian tribes (the ones mentioned in poetry in this book are the Kwakiutls of British Columbia; the Haidas and Tlingits of Alaska) was the leisure time afforded them by the plentitude of fresh food from the sea. The supply was unlimited and varied from whale to smelt and from halibut to seal. The Indians of this region did not have to wander or wonder where their next meal was coming from, for everything of bounty came from the limitless ocean. In the midst of such graciousness came furs which the white traders and traders from the East prized and, in addition, some of the finest and most decorative art in wood, copper, slate, basketry, and clothing that the world has ever seen. Nonetheless, the world of the Northwest Coast was not without its intimation of danger. Tribes fought bitterly over the sites to found their villages and this was one of the few places in North America where land was at a premium within the Indian culture itself. Thus war carried a devastating premium: it emphasized the right to live more than the will to conquer. The game of courting honor and counting coups by attacking a warring tribe, so common in the Plains tribes, was uncommon in the Northwest where war was a bitter business designed to eliminate a contestant for space.

PEOPLE OF THE DESERT

THEY CROSSED OVER

They came to the place
that was to be a Katchina
village.
The brother desired the sister.
When the wind came up,
it raised her apron of grass.
She lay sleeping.
He desired her.
He lay down on his sister
and his sister woke up.
"Oh no!" she said, "You."
He made a river
with his big toe.
All the People came.
"It will be all right for you
to cross over here," he said.
The People entered the river;
some of their children turned
into watersnakes.
Some into turtles,
frogs, lizards.

They bit their mothers
who cried out and dropped them.
Then the People were told
not to drop the water-babies;
the brother and sister
who made love told them this.
He said, "Hold on even
when they bite and scratch."
And the People crossed over
with a lot of biting
and scratching going on
and they cried out
and didn't drop them.
And the creatures quieted
down.
And that is how they crossed over.

Zuni

MEDITATION ON CROSSING OVER

This story is told many ways by many tribal storytellers. Not exclusively Zuni, although that is its source here. In the beginning, a crossing-over place. Becoming later, in the time of the telling of legends, a sacred place, a place of Katchinas. Brother and sister are origin figures. They have godlike nature, but are human and make mistakes. Making love on their journey is incestuous and causes the babies to go crazy and to act as wildness dictates, biting and scratching. When the People, the first people of the tribe, lose heart and drop them, Brother and Sister admonish: Courage, Hold On, Be Strong. The People obey, the crossing is made safely. Is there a moral line here? Do Brother and Sister show misconduct? Does power of guidance fail in the first crossing over because of mistaken lovemaking? Is Courage the highest virtue—cancelling all error?

The babies become creatures and in the final crossing are made calm. Later that illuminated waterplace is the underworld home of the Katchinas, supernatural power force of the Zuni people. Through a kind of non-reaction good occurs. The Chinese Taoists say, "Follow the Way that is always there." In the creature world there is inherent calm. The stalking cat, the about-to-be-killed-mouse know it, deeply. Man learns it. He must cross over.

SANTO DOMINGO CORN DANCE

Fading parrot-feathered hair
  skunk-furred feet
  old men in fat skin
  made young by clay.

Hollow-heart drum dies from
  light-foot girls
  sprigs of pine
  tranced in rain.

Hundreds of dusted dancers
  mothers, daughters, sisters
  —seedlings and cones—
  soaking old drum
  in summer rain.

Santo Domingo Pueblo

MEDITATION ON
SANTO DOMINGO CORN DANCE

On or around August fourth, the dance takes place. It
is a great dance, one of the best of its kind in the
Southwest. The entire pueblo gathers under the portals
of mud-baked adobes. But this is not so. The entire
pueblo—it now truly seems—is marching up the narrow corridor between ancient buildings. Now the wind
and dust and dance begin. Eyes are dizzied by the
stamp and turn of so many children, young people,
men and women and old ones. The pueblo is rocked
with the sound of male feet coming down hard,
female feet rising and falling, the two alternating as
the drum insists the earth is alive, the sky waiting.
Always the pause between the feet and the drum when
the breath of the earth seems to be sucked in, holds,
breathes, and the controlled thunder rolls out its
enduring pace.

You sit, if willing, all day until the faces of dancers and
singers and koshare are known intimately. The drums
and dancers master the mountains and overcome the
dry plains, the insufferable heat, the stinging flies.
Bread is passed round, golden loaves of sun.

The sun hides behind clouds; real thunder rolls out of
the sky. In moments, the bread still moist in the
mouth, the rain coming in sheets, then driving nails.
The dancers, fox-skinned, parrot-feathered, disappear
in a blaze of dazzling rain. Suddenly the crowds are
gone, the dancers gone; all but the rain, which is now
the drum that was beating all day, gone. This drum,
the answering one, is female and nourishes corn.

DAWN STEALER

Old Coyote, dawn stealer
in the first days of life,
howling at the center
of all things dark
with his mocking heart—
   laughing, laughing
     at the sun—
a memory too hot
to hold
on even
his tricky tongue.

     Navajo

MEDITATION ON DAWN STEALER

Coyote remembers all. He is one in wisdom with
koshare, pueblo clown, because in his daring stance,
his fumbling foolishness, his love of the poetry of non-
sense, things begin anew, things are fun again, for all.
But not without danger or trickery. Stories of Coyote:
how he got his yellow eyes, how he tried to have spots
like baby deer, how he drank too much wine, got sick,
how he tricked giants, proved he could take pain.
These endless stories, seasonal cycles.

One day camping on a mesa, miles from anywhere,
Coyote actually spoke to me. Dawn: no one awake
except myself and this dual presence of dog-and-man,
not more than a few feet away from the campsite. The
Navajo next to me slept soundly. When I woke him so
he could hear what Coyote was saying, he said "Go
back to sleep and leave Coyote alone." I sat up as the
sky got red and listened to the beauty of that solitary
voice. Later that day Ray said, "He was just telling you
how he stole the sun once, but even Coyote couldn't
keep hold of it." I said, "There was laughter in that
voice, all the mischief of life." He said, unamused, "He
knows that better than anyone."

OWL BOY

He was born with the wide eyes
of an owl.
His hands were long and his fingers
were tapered
and he was fond of grasping things.

His mother was afraid of him
and she hung him in a tree
and he was taken away
at night
to live with the owl people.

He learned to fly low over the hills
and to tear the air
with his cry.
With his fingers he could tear
meat from bones.

One day he sought his parents.
He traveled after moonrise
and he found their last home.
Under the smoke hole an old corncob
in the dead fire spoke to him.

"Look," it said, "they have gone away,
they are not here anymore."
Owl Boy took to wing
and he followed their trail,
for he was anxious to meet his other parents.

When he found them, they were
at a big dance, the whole tribe
was there.
Owl Boy cried, "Mother, Father,"
but his voice was of the Owl People.

The mother and father were frightened
and they ran from their son.
When they found he was everywhere
in the air around them,
they shot arrows at him.

Owl Boy flew upon them swiftly, angrily.
He tore at them with his claws.
With his wide night-seeing eyes
he saw them: they were his parents,
but they were afraid and he killed them.

And Owl Boy went back to his own People,
to the land of the owl.

Navajo/Apache

MEDITATION ON OWL BOY

Originally, the Navajos and Apaches were as one. Owl
Boy was a tribal member before becoming an owl person. Today, Navajo human babies are still said to be
born with characteristics of animals. Faces lightly
furred, mouths shaped to fit sharp canine teeth, large
nocturnal eyes like Owl Boy's. The power of the dark
world is one with us, it is within. When we deny its
power as the parents of Owl Boy, we bring vengeance
upon us. Owls are ghosts of the departed to the
Navajo, as well as messengers of the other world, and
they are often shunned. The hogan, after the dead
who lived in it are buried, is burned, all vestiges of
ownership including tracks brushed away, so that the
dead cannot come back and haunt the living. Owl Boy
is the emissary from the dead's world. In white culture
these emissaries are monsters; we are afraid of them.
Navajos and Apaches are also afraid. But there is this
difference. Owl Boy does not seek his human family to
betray or wreak vengeance upon them, only to meet
and be with them. He acknowledges them as his
human counterparts with whom he must have spiritual
contact along with his owl parents. Rejected, he
becomes like any human animal—vengeful. Rejected,
he kills his parents. The link between the two worlds is
broken.

SKIN WALKER

Out of the brittle shell, by starlight
wolf fur on pale skin

The scents come back
soft hands leave hard paw treads

By dawn, the frayed magic
stuffed in a hollow tree

The scary daylight reminds us
we are all
HE WHO WALKS IN SKINS

naked, alone
furred, in packs

Navajo

MEDITATION ON SKIN WALKER

A late fall night. I was told: That man is a Skin Walker.
First hearing of the name. They are men who become
wolves for the purpose of doing evil. A medicine man,
Navajo, showed how to protect against their comings
and goings. They move very quickly, he said, faster
than cars; they can be in two places at once. They
need never lift a finger to perform their deeds. In a
Squaw Dance performed in the Enemy Way to protect
a man from some uncertain evil that was stalking him,
some sheep were killed. The sheep were killed in the
traditional way for the feast after the dance, but the
man whose luck was down for whom the dance was
held, forgot himself, forgot the necessity of watching
each small thing in life, bringing harmony to it; he sold
the hides of those sheep to a white trader. Immedi-
ately, the Skin Walker stalking him did away with half
his herd of sheep. Slaughtered in a demonic way. By
accident, the luckless man, cleaning his rifle at home,
fired a shot which nearly killed his daughter. Later, the
man himself almost died of an unknown illness. The
poem "Skin Walker" tells how a man of flesh and
blood hides his skin-walking presence in the hollow of
a tree. He needs night to do his work; the mantle of
protective darkness. In the poem the meaning reaches
out to each of us—who among us, Indian or white, can
say "I am free of the darkness that covers all?"

PRAYER FOR RED MEAT

One night
when Old Moon
was a bone awl
in a moccasin bag of stars
I dreamt of horns,
sang them in my sleep.

Then the white dream of an arrow
was my own hunger.

Sing thanks for bone, fat, meat
and thong.

Sing praise: my heart, my song.

Anasazi

MEDITATION ON RED MEAT AND PRAYER

A person who does not sing praise does not know
his/her mind. Praise is also at the heart of things. The
moccasin bag of stars—what we might call the Taoistic
flow of the universe, or simply the Tao—and the
dreams in a person's life are not personal gratifications
of glory or good luck, but perfect synchronicity of life
when understood, when all things stand in balance
with one another. Native American history's full of
dream prophecy, good and bad. Men or women who
possess this quality are shamans, blessed with knowing
the outcome of events before they occur. But are these
people different from others of the tribe? Yes and no.
The others also practice foreknowledge, for that is
what a hunter does to propitiate the hunt, what a
dancer does before the dance is initiated. A dream
says: Deer will be at a certain place at a certain time; a
man goes there and it is done. The man gives thanks,
sings praise with heart and song. These things woven
into the fabric and form of a lifetime. A Thai poet said,
speaking in understatement of the enormity of hunger
in his country: "To eat you must have food." The
American Indian said, "To eat you must have prayer."
To pray, you must have dreams.

Navajo, Apache, Pueblo; tribes of the great Southwest, mountain-traveling, mesa-dwelling, far-seeing people of the high desert. It is believed the Navajos and the Apaches were once one tribe, a tribe that split apart and went separate yet similar ways. Sand paintings for healing are done by both and their nomadic ways, coming with the dust and going with the wind, explain much of the discontent of their lives when, towards the end of the nineteenth century, they were forcibly reservation bound.

Navajo land is located today in that area known as the Four Corners, covering the high dry desert region of Colorado, New Mexico, Arizona, and Utah. Apache country now comprises New Mexico, southern and northern boundaries, and Arizona. Most of the major Pueblo villages of the Southwest are found near the Rio Grande in New Mexico. There are nineteen Pueblo villages: northern, southern, and western. Their great similarity is that unlike the Navajos and Apaches, the Pueblos were deeply rooted in the soil and sand of their particular hemisphere.

The Pueblo villages of the Rio Grande are very old, descendants perhaps of the even older and now vanished ancestral villages of the Anasazi, or *ancient ones*. Pueblo culture reflects an eternal flow and rootedness of one place; their weaving and silverwork were already highly developed when the first Navajo and Apache raiding parties feathered the river hills of northern New Mexico. Warriors and raiders, the Navajos (Apaches de Nabaju, as they were originally called by the early Spanish explorers) took *artforms* along with stolen women when they pillaged the Pueblos. Somehow, as a result, the Navajos, more than any other Southwestern tribe, became the most versatile and the best weavers and silverworkers in the country. Today, despite massive epidemics over the centuries and other setbacks including constant depredations of the white man, the Nabajoos, Nabajus, Navajos, or Navahos have flourished as the largest indigenous culture in the United States.

PEOPLE OF THE PLAINS

WINTER COUNTS OF THE DAKOTAS

I: MANY EAGLES CATCHING WINTER

Man who digs hole and covers himself
reaches out when eagle falls
and takes eagle by feet—
this man *is* an eagle,
now joined are head and claw!

II: WOMAN INSIDE BUFFALO WINTER

One says old woman eaten by monster buffalo;
One says old squaw out in cold
hides inside buffalo carcass to keep warm;
One says woman inside buffalo means
something altogether different,
something from religion;
One says all these were told to a White Man
and therefore none are true.

III: BUFFALO COME CLOSE TO TIPI WINTER

Half-moon hoof mark: not horse.
Buffalo visit winter.
Many come, you see them at your door.
We haven't worries.

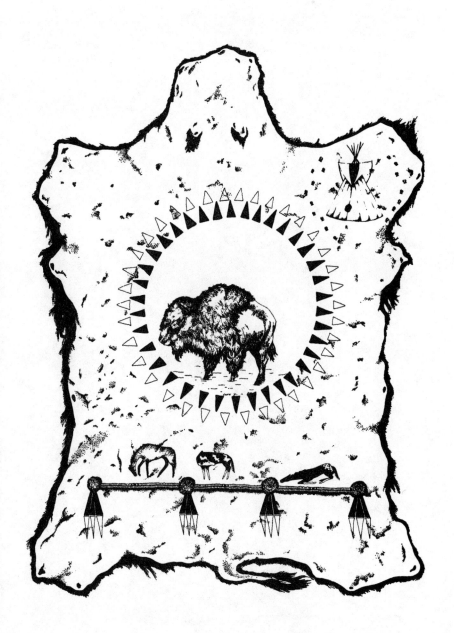

IV: MANY HORSES DIE IN SNOW WINTER

Many horses die for lack of grass.
Unable to eat snow
unable to paw through it,
they are given away to winter
as if they never had an owner.

V: LITTLE SWAN DIES ON CHERRY CREEK WINTER

Swan flies south with man;
man flies south with swan.

MEDITATION ON WINTER COUNTS

Time was reckoned by the Dakotas in terms of winters, executed on hides in colors, and often presented in spiral form, the shape of a snail's shell. Winter counts grew, secreted by time, rather than added or made by men; they were an integral reality of time itself, not an artificial construction. Winter counts depict, in many cases, images that move in time from left to right. In this way, they can be linked to Chinese ideograms. These poems are bare essences because they reflect images rather than words. In fact, putting them into words is a "captional" way of showing their original intent.

These particular winter counts begin in 1806 and end in 1867; the progression is indicated by the order in which they are placed in the book. In each case, or count, we see a joining of man and nature into inseparability. Little Swan, the warrior, shown arms out-stretched: in death, in battle, in flight. The name given him in this life is his power; in the next it continues to aid him, to wing him into the spirit world. Spirituality of the swan is without question one of the highest in white culture, as well as Oriental and Native American.

Missing woman—swallowed by a giant buffalo?—is an interesting motif. Dakotas did believe in giants, animal and human, because among other things, remains of actual giants—dinosaurs, mammoths, bisons—were scattered about the great plains of their homeland. Men and women sought refuge in warm bodies of freshly killed animals in times of desperation. But these are logical answers. The swan is part of the head of the warrior—buffaloes and people interchange iden-tities. Why should one not give birth to the other? Why should a woman not carry a little buffalo in her womb; why should a buffalo not carry a little woman?

SKINS

1

The longsnake dotted with yellow spots,
    the bullsnake.
Above the bunches of tall grass,
    he lives.
And even though a man dies
    and passes into the realm of spirits,
through his strength they shall recover.

2

The great snake that makes a buzzing
    sound makes a sound like the blowing
of the wind—close to the feet of the sick—
    sounding his rattle close to the head
of the sick—sounding his rattle—
        toward the east winds
        toward the west winds
        towards the winds from the cedars
into the days of peace and beauty
when men make of me their bodies
into the days of peace and beauty
that will come.

3

I am fitted for the use of men
who want to reach old age.
Behold the skin of my feet
I have made the means
to reach old age.

Behold the skin of my feet
dark as charcoal—
when men make of these feet
their own charcoal
it will easily sink into their skin.

Behold the tip of my black beak—
this as charcoal will seep
deeply into their skins.

Behold my tail and my other black
body parts—when the little men
make of me their bodies—
they will have charcoal
that will easily sink
into their skin.

4

I am the male puma who lies
upon the earth.
I am a person who had made a
male puma of his body.
The knowledge of my courage
has spread over the land.
The god of day sits in the heavens.
I sit close to the god of day.
When men make me their god,
all deaths die
as they travel the paths of life.

Osage

A PERSON

I am a person never absent
from any important act.
Great Elk is the name I have taken.
When men hunt little animals
I will always make them appear
to them.
In the midst of each of the four
winds, I throw myself upon the earth.
I cleanse all the land of my anger.
I throw myself and leave the hairs
of my body—these hairs I have
scattered so that animals may
appear in their midst, they are
the grasses of this earth.
I have made the grasses
so the animals may appear
so you may live
upon the earth
upon the earth.

Osage

MEDITATION ON SKINS

What munificent spirit guides the actions of all
things? In "Skins" the snakes, winds, and cedars are
made into the days of beauty. Men are no less beauti-
ful than animals. Men, in fact, are animals. Special animals. "I am fitted for the use of men who want to reach
old age." It is the snake, the puma, the elk, the eagle
inhabiting the winds and cedars that make men fit to
live long. From them we learn our stride. We sit up
nights. We have cold skin; we wear theirs. "I am the
person never absent from any important act." The elk
is the person. He will teach us. "I cleanse the land of
anger." Only when anger is cleansed is wisdom born.
Look: the animals do not make war. The great snake
sounds his rattle, but he does not make war on any but
the white man. When the elk, the puma, the eagle are
gone, there will be left the People. And what will they
do, those few who live on? It is history's turn to
answer—"It is the People who are eliminated first."
These words, this book of animal meditations, these
are the last words before the flood of men and the
drowning of the People. There are no voices left, and
the animals too are dying out; kept on for the pleasure
of men, but dying out. Where are the ghosts who said
these words, who left these tracks, who palmed their
message on canyon walls?

Of the plain, of the great open spaces—they are quite commonly the Native Americans chosen for the white man's myth-making: the noblest of noble savages. Characteristic of these people, thought romantics of the nineteenth century, was their freedom, their decorative clothing, their unity with the horse. However, it was not always so. The Dakotans, whom the whites still think of as the tipi-dwelling, buffalo-hunting warriors of time immemorial, were part of a great Siouan family. It is from this name that we got the tribal name: Sioux.

Before the coming of the white man, before the advent of the horse, the Sioux were simply a group of closely related woodland tribes living west of the Chippewas in Wisconsin. The Sioux enjoyed gardening and the extent of their buffalo hunting was the occasional adventure in the Great Plains. In time, though, they were pushed out toward the Plains by the Chippewa. The easy mobility of the horse made possible a nomadic hunting life. With the horse also came the means with which to make war and a reason (horse-stealing) to perpetuate it.

The Osage people lived originally on the Little Osage River near its confluence with the main Osage River of Missouri. They too were members of the Siouan family and their kindred tribes were the Omaha, Ponca, Quapaw, and Kaw. Their present home in Osage County, Oklahoma proved mineral-rich and yielded oil, oil royalties, and oil scandals. For once, the irony played against the white man: land that was considered undesirable yielded much wealth to non-white owners who had been forcibly moved from their old reservation in Kansas.

PEOPLE OF THE PLANET

THE BOY WITH THE SUN TREE BOW

In the beginning the sea was a true-blue eye
with the sun in the center by day
and the moon in the corner by night.

Bright fish swam in and out of the sun.
Dark turtles crossed over the moon
and all was well in the world.

Then came a boy with a bow
whose dream was to shoot out
the sun and the moon
with a single arrow.

Day after day he bent his bow
toward the sky, but each time
the string snapped
the bow broke
the arrow flew untrue.

"There must be something wrong
with the curve of my bow,
the wood of my arrow," the boy thought.

And he tried plum, elm, pine, pear,
cherry, maple, beech, hickory, oak, ash—
but none would give him
the curved bow, the straight arrow he needed.

One day he found a tree
in a little clearing
and it had sprung branches and twiny roots
and the fruit of this tree
hung in the air like fallen suns.
Next to this tree was another
and its limbs were long and smooth
with shapely roots
and the fruit of this tree
was like round silken moons.

In the sun tree gold bees—lion-headed
and maned—roared and hummed
and bore through their hives.

In the moon tree furred moths
with silver eyes and breezy wings
drank from the petals of moonflower nectar.

Seeing the two trees, the boy drove away
the bees and the moths
by fanning thick smoke into their leaves
and he felled the two trees
with a double-edged axe.

From the sun tree he carved an incredible bow
that would bend round as the seasons of the sun.
From the moon tree he shaved a flexible arrow
that would glow quick as the curve of the moon.
And the boy lay down in the grass
on his back by the side of the sea
and he bent his bow
until golden beads popped out of the wood
and he fingered the moth-wing feather ends
of the sleek arrow, held them true to the sun—
and let go.

The moment the arrow left the bow
the sun and the moon shone black
at opposite ends of the sky
and the earth burned bright as a comet
and the boy heard every living thing
vanish from the earth like a bow string—
Zing!

Every bark shred, grassblade, acorn shell—
Zing!
Every flower, mushroom, molehill, meadow—
Zing!
Every pebble, twig, tadpole, turnip—
Zing!
Every rabbit, squirrel, turtle,
fly, flea, frog,
rat, cricket, cow,
badger, buffalo, baboon, boy—
Zing!

In the beginning the sea was a true·blue eye
with the sun in the center by day
and the moon in the corner by night.
Bright fish swam in and out of the sun,
dark turtles crossed over the moon
and all was well with the world.

CONCLUSION: MEDITATION ON BOY WITH THE SUN TREE BOW

This poem came both from the depth of my subconscious and from my own Native American geneology. Written in the dead of night, it came first on the wings of a dream. I was frightened by it—by what it implied. The life of any poem is its own, and this one has had several lives beyond the control of its author. In the mid-seventies the poem had two stage appearances as a free form or interpretive dance. Its first performance was in Stockbridge, Massachusetts where it was subsequently issued as a children's book by Berkshire Traveller Press. A second dance performance was sponsored in Pittsfield, Massachusetts by the Massachusetts Society for the Prevention of Cruelty to Children. Accompanied by a bamboo flute and an interpretive dancer from the Juilliard School of Music, the poem appeared as liquid sound, voice theater, rippling movement of a single dancer's body; the dance, the voice, the flute, the poem were a success. It was later given radio life and sponsored by state humanities grants as well as National Endowment funding, and read to scores of college and university students.

Now it is time to free the poem again and to allow it to speak in another kind of way. The message of the poet is clearly directed toward an anti-nuclear stance. The people of this planet are all natives of life, free to make the subconscious choice of birth over death, beauty over disharmony, global peace over universal liquidation. It is not too late to free the Boy from his mindless act.

How many tribes in the course of Native American history have shot arrows to the sun? Each tribe has its own version of the wish to reach Father Sun and

Mother Moon—to unite with them, to learn and then
return and to teach men of this celestial knowledge.
Gerald McDermott's *Arrow to the Sun*, a Zuni tale, and
The Angry Moon, retold by William Sleator with pic-
tures by Blair Lent, are two such examples which are
always worth reexamining, both for the vivid illustrations and the poignant moral expressing our indebted-
ness to the world around us, our need to
communicate, to offer prayer and obeisance to the sun
and the moon. An adult version of this interlinear wish
to be enjoined in prayer with the infinite as expressed
by the Sun Father is well documented by Robert Bois-
siere in his text *Po Pai Mo: The Search for White
Buffalo Woman*.

I offer my own version in the following way: The
wish, the dream, are our greatness. Hal Borland said in
When the Legends Die—"When the dreams end, there
is no more greatness." But the dream must not over-
step natural bounds. The egotism of the Boy must not
surpass the wish to become one with the infinite. In the
heart of the Boy—at first—is the unselfish wish to
touch. To reach out. Then he employs ingenuity and
art in his reaching, and his ego grows. Then his wish
turns into a passion, to outfire the sun—to equal Sun
Father with his own personal power, and to fire down
the moon, his Mother. In reaching too far, he punishes
the entire race. He turns his ego into a conflagration.
As a result, we are doomed to be lost in the space of
our own misjudgement, and thus to sacrifice our
unique but not separate place in the firmament. Such
an event would truly exemplify humanity's fall from
grace. Let us hope this is not the only way we may
learn to follow our psychic urge to join the process of
the cosmos. Let us hope that the era when male and

female principles, which governed the life of men and women on Turtle Island for hundreds of years before the appearance of the white man, is near at hand. For it is in the collaboration of the sexes that human energy is irradiated and ultimately sustained on this planet. It is not too late to abandon the "boy" in each of us and instead to trust the ripened wisdom of the man-woman, woman-man, the *Wu-men*. When we say the word *women* in English, we are saying simultaneously in Chinese: *wu* and *men*. Wu meaning *without*, men meaning *door* or *gate*. So saying we have a union born of opposites: the "gateless gate" in Chinese is called *Wu Men Kuan*. It is the way without the way, the door of no door, the knowledge without knowledge. As the "boy"—that destructive impulse of ego-nature—is lifted from our midst, we embrace and pull the bow of beauty, letting fly the arrow of our deepest psychic dream—unity with the cosmos, freedom from self, *wu men kuan*, the gateless gate to the universe.

Afterword: Body-Spirit-Being

The poems and meditations in this book are the essence of a reality that arises from the communion of the human spirit with its non-human "otherness" that co-inheres in animals and Nature, and gains expression in animism and mythic imagery. This communion, which seems "primitive" from an anthropocentric perspective, does not objectify animals and Nature as something separate, even alien, if not inferior. Rather, they are *incorporated:* That which is incorporated—recognized and felt as part of one's own body-spirit-being—cannot be harmed or defiled without harming one's self. We can only destroy and desecrate that which we objectify. Ecocide, "speciesicide," genocide, and suicide are one and the same. There is no separation. Aside from this enlightened view of survival and creation, there is a deeper wisdom and humility that are the gifts of understanding animals, plants, and the rhythms and cycles of life and Nature. Without this understanding, human life becomes disconnected. This is often manifested as *dis-ease*, rather than ease, which is a symptom of what the Hopis call *Koyaanasquatsi*—Life out of balance.

We have almost lost contact with that part of ourselves which resonates with other animals and with Nature. It is that part of ourselves that enables us to experience the spiritual unity of our own being with all beings and to know intuitively that we and all life are of the same origin and Creation. The objective knowledge of the modern sciences of ecology, evolutionary biology, and ethology confirm this intuitive wisdom, leading to an empathetic appreciation and understanding of animals and Nature and of our place in the world that are essential prerequisites to humane planetary stewardship and to our health and overall well-being.

We have been slow to learn that such objective and instrumental knowledge becomes destructive when it is applied primarily to gain power and control over Nature, the animal kingdom, and the creative process. The unity, connectedness, wholeness—and holiness—of Creation are then disturbed and the sacred order and harmony defiled and desecrated. This misuse of our power of dominion has now reached the point where the creative process itself (through biotechnology and other scientific-industrial innovations) is being directed to satisfy exclusively human ends. The fundamental motivation and goal is security, which is manifested as the desire for ever greater profits, growth, progress, efficiency, and military invincibility. This is the *ethos* of a technocratic and highly anthropocentric world view that is turning nature into an industrialized, poisoned wasteland. It is also responsible for the holocaust of the animal kingdom and for much human suffering, including famine, drought, floods, epidemics of cancer, birth defects, and even war over dwindling world resources.

The irony and tragedy of this world view is that it is blind to its own nemesis. Its negative consequences intensify our collective insecurity. This insecurity, which intensifies the quest for absolute power and control, is compounded by a deeper existential insecurity that the technocratic, anthropocentric world view creates by disconnecting us from the essential, non-dualistic unity of body/soul; matter/spirit; human/animal; humanity/earth; nature/divinity.

The dualistic world view is alienating and objectifying; animals, humans, and Nature become expendable resources whose exploitation is justified for the "greater good" of society. This has its roots arguably in our Western culture, in the Protestant Work Ethic. And it has been given religious sanction by a perverse materialistic belief system that masquerades as Christianity and which interprets the word dominion (Genesis 1:26) as a God-given right to dominate and exploit all of God's creation for purely human ends. By so doing, its adherents commit the cardinal sin of *hubris,* of assuming dominion over God. This pathological state, with its destructive, alienating, and anxiety-evoking consequences, is imbued with a sense of meaninglessness. Indeed, the production and proliferation of ever more material goods, scientific knowledge for knowledge's sake, and industrial growth for growth's sake are means that have become ends in themselves. The futility and meaninglessness of a purely materialistic, instrumental, technocratic society arise from an inherent lack of non-materialistic, ecological, and spiritual values. These have been supplanted by a utopian goal of technological progress and industrial growth that today has the impetus of the Bible's paradisiacal vision of a millenium to come akin to a new Golden Age. While we cannot blame science, technology and industry for the destruction of Nature and the holocaust of the animal kingdom, we cannot ignore the fact that the possibility of a Golden Age to come seems ever more remote. This is because we have almost destroyed that part of ourselves that resonates with other animals and Nature—the heart of compassion—through the emotive and spiritual connection we know as empathy.

It is through the "mediumship" of the artist, mystic poet, and shaman that we begin to resonate again with Nature and fellow creature beings; and become reconnected, healed, made whole and thus experience all that is holy. "At-onement" is atonement. Realizing the unity and interdependence of all life, we discover the sacred nature and significance of our connections, and then spontaneously act with conscience, treating all of life with reverence. In this state of being-in-the-world, consciously aware of our connections with the rest of creation, we cannot harm or hurt anything without doing so to ourselves. This is the "burden" of empathy, compassion's bridge. And since we and all living things are part of the one life, compassion becomes unconditional, boundless, and absolute. All living things and non-living entities of God's creation are then treated with humility and given equal and fair consideration. This *metanoia* entails a transformation from a dualistic and anthropocentric world view to a theocentric or creation-centered cosmology. Then, and only then, can science, technology, and industry be applied non-destructively. Without such a transformation we lack the empathetic sensitivity, intuitive wisdom, and ethical sensibility essential for our *creative* participation, as humane planetary stewards, in the nurturing and unfoldment of life on Earth.

The environmental and other crises that we face today, and the holocaust of the animal and plant kingdoms, properly apprehended, are Nature's way of telling us that if we are to survive and prosper, we must change our ways and our world view. We cannot survive long or prosper at the expense of environmental quality violating the absolute right of all life to a whole and healthy biosphere.

Gerald Hausman's *Meditations With Animals* is an important book because in reconnecting that part of ourselves which resonates with other animals and with Nature, a sense of wonder and reverence for all life is awakened. Such awakening is a revelation, not simply of this poet's skill and sensitivity, but also of our own nature, power, and inherent divinity which we discover when we experience these same omnipresent qualities in Nature, and all creation.

Dr. Michael W. Fox
Scientific Director
The Humane Society of the United States
Washington, D.C.

Publisher's Note:

Bear & Company is publishing this series of creation-centered mystic/prophets to bring to the attention and prayer of peoples today the power and energy of the holistic mystics of the western tradition. One reason western culture succumbs to boredom and to violence is that we are not being challenged by our religious traditions to be all we can be. This is also the reason that many sincere spiritual seekers go East for their mysticism—because the West is itself out of touch with its deepest spiritual guides. The format Bear & Company has chosen in which to present these holistic mystic/prophets is deliberate: We do not feel that more academically-styled books on our mystics is what every-day believers need. Rather, we wish to get the mystics of personal and social transformation off our dusty shelves and into the hearts and minds and bodies of our people. To do this we choose a format that is ideal for meditation, for imaging, for sharing in groups and in prayer occasions. We rely on primary sources for the texts but we let the author's words and images flow from her or his inner structure to our deep inner selves.

Other Books in the

MEDITATIONS WITH™
Series

Meister Eckhart
Dante Alighieri
Hildegard of Bingen
Hopis
Julian of Norwich
Mechtild of Magdeburg
Native Americans: Lakota Spirituality
Teresa of Avila

Contact your local bookseller
or write:

Bear & Company, Inc.
PO Drawer 2860
Santa Fe, NM 87504